W9-BLT-144

# The Majesty of New Orleans

# The Majesty of
# NEW ORLEANS

Photography by Paul Malone
Text by Lee Malone

PELICAN PUBLISHING COMPANY
Gretna 1998

Copyright © 1992
By Lee and Paul Malone
All rights reserved

First printing, 1992
Second printing, 1998
First paperback edition, 1998

---

*The word "Pelican" and the depiction of a pelican are trademarks of Pelican Publishing Company, Inc., and are registered in the U.S. Patent and Trademark Office.*

---

**Library of Congress Cataloging-in-Publication Data**

Malone, Paul.
    The majesty of New Orleans / photography by Paul Malone; text by Lee Malone.
        p.   cm.
    Includes bibliographical references.
    ISBN 0-88289-863-9 (hc : alk. paper) — ISBN 1-56554-377-7 (pbk. : alk. paper)
    1. New Orleans (La.)—Description—Guide-books. 2. New Orleans (La.)—Description—Views. 3. Architecture—Louisiana—New Orleans—Guide-books. I. Malone, Lee. II. Title.
    F379.N53M35 1992
    917.63'350463—dc20                                                91-29043
                                                                        CIP

*Photo on p. 2: Loeber House.*
*Photo on p. 6: Courtyard of the John Gauché House.*
*Photo on p. 8: Gibson Hall of Tulane University.*

Book design by Dana Bilbray

Printed in Singapore

Published by Pelican Publishing Company, Inc.
P.O. Box 3110, Gretna, Louisiana 70054-3110

*We dedicate this book to Michael M. Pilié,
who is always there with his enthusiasm, suggestions, and
inspiration when they are needed.*

# Contents

# Acknowledgments

Dr. Milburn and Nancy Calhoun of Pelican Publishing Company for their much appreciated interest and assistance.

Louis and Joni Darré and the personnel of their organization, Professional Color Laboratory, for their invaluable technical assistance.

The Historic New Orleans Collection for their research facilities, and their dedicated, knowledgeable, and pleasant staff.

# Introduction

The thriving, fascinating city of New Orleans was once a dismal, brooding swampland at the mouth of the Mississippi River.

Courage and fortitude had to be mustered by the first European settlers in order to withstand the floods, hurricanes, and diseases that nature inflicted upon the struggling colony. The settlement was below sea level, flanked by Lake Pontchartrain and the Mississippi River, and constantly in danger of floods. In the springtime, mosquitoes from the wetlands invaded the hapless town. The *Aedes agypti* mosquito carried the dreaded yellow fever, of which many of the colonists died.

Through perseverance, in 1810 the city's first waterworks was established. In 1905 yellow fever was conquered. In 1914 the land was drained of excess water and New Orleans became a healthful, vibrant community.

The main thoroughfare, Canal Street, at one time intended to be an open canal, divides two distinctly different parts of the city. Upriver from it is referred to as "uptown," the newer section, and downriver from it is "downtown," the older section. The 171-foot-wide boulevard begins at the river and ends fifty blocks away where several cemeteries are located.

Shopping centers in other parts of the city now augment the main shopping area, which begins at the river and continues on Canal Street for approximately fifteen blocks. Until recently four streetcar lines connected the central section to outlying areas. However, the St. Charles Avenue line is the only original route remaining.

The St. Charles Avenue streetcar was put in service as a steamcar on September 26, 1825. The line was electrified on February 1, 1893. It was named the St. Charles Avenue Belt on February 19, 1900, because the route encircled a part of the city. (From Canal Street it went up St. Charles Avenue, turned at Carrollton, and traveled back to Canal Street.) In 1951, on January 8, the route was changed again and it was called the St. Charles Avenue line, as it is today.

Business and financial districts, better homes, and two universities are established in uptown New Orleans. St. Charles Avenue, its main street, follows the crescent of the river.

The Vieux Carré (French Quarter), on the downtown side of Canal Street, is little changed by the years. A maze of ancient and exquisite architecture, French and Spanish in style and adorned with delicate iron filigree, is viewed with pleasure. Countless sunny courtyards, antique shops, bookstores, and excellent restaurants fill the area.

New Orleanians are a fun-loving people. Throughout the uphill battle to attain a pleasant way of life, they enjoyed the opera and Mardi Gras activities. Today the gaiety continues. It has been said that the local people will parade at the drop of a hat. Actually, the hat doesn't have to touch the ground before the die is cast and another parade is planned.

Visitors to the city are amazed at the variety of recreational entertainments. They delight in attending the theater, visiting the festivals, sailing on the lake, or strolling through the aquarium and the zoo. Carnival balls and Mardi Gras Day highlight each year.

Of captivating contrasts, New Orleans is indeed one of the most interesting cities in the United States.

# The Majesty of New Orleans

*A side view of the United States Mint.*

# Architecture

The architecture of New Orleans consists of a mixture of several styles: Creole cottages, sometimes constructed of *briquette-entre-poteaux* (brick between posts); the two-story house with a side hall plan which shows Anglo-American influence; the raised villa, one and one-half story, five bay, gallery-fronted houses with Greek or Renaissance Revival details; the single or double shotgun with late Renaissance Revival or Eastlake details, reflecting Victorian towers, bays, and asymmetry, as well as elaborate decoration; and the early twentieth century eclectic bungalow, Colonial Revival or Mission-style structures.

Two disastrous fires in 1788 and 1794 almost destroyed the *Vieux Carré,* which was rebuilt with more elaborate houses. Therefore, most of the existing historic buildings in that area date from the nineteenth century.

Significantly important Colonial-period structures and many later houses designed to abut one another are found in the French Quarter. Some are two or three stories topped by simple gables. Others are one-story single or double Creole cottages.

The houses in the Faubourg (suburb) Marigny area are predominantly one- or two-story Creole cottages. There are, however, some excellent examples of Greek Revival, Victorian, and Edwardian architecture, as well as twentieth century buildings in this area too.

The Garden District, mainly a residential area, contains domestic architecture dating from 1835 to 1860 with several different styles including Gothic, Greek Revival, and Italianate.

A large part of the Irish Channel area is characterized by dwellings which make maximum use of their lots, usually with a small front yard, a narrow alleyway on each side, and a back yard. This type of house was called a "shotgun." It often consisted of a double parlor followed by three other rooms. These became known as "shotgun houses" because the rooms were *en suite,* each room following the other in a straight line. It was humorously said that if one stood at the front door and shot a pistol, the shot would go through the house and exit through the back door. When the back two rooms were repeated on a second floor, the house was called a "camelback."

13

## Longue Vue House and Gardens
### *#7 Bamboo Road*

Mr. and Mrs. Edgar Stern, builders of Longue Vue House and Gardens, now open to the public, gave of themselves to enrich the lives of others.

Edgar Stern was awarded the *Times-Picayune* Loving Cup in 1930. This award, given annually to individuals "who have served the New Orleans area in civic, business, religious, or cultural areas without expectation of reward or recognition," was also given to Mrs. Stern thirty-four years later, in 1964, making the Sterns the only husband and wife so honored.

After Mr. Stern's death in 1959, Mrs. Stern maintained her residence at Longue Vue until 1978. It was not surprising that before her death in 1980 one of her final philanthropic gestures was to create a nonprofit foundation to maintain her house and gardens for the public to enjoy.

## Pitot House
### 1440 Moss Street

James Pitot bought this house with its thirty-acre sugarcane plantation in 1810. He had already attained prominence in New Orleans by establishing himself as a commission merchant and serving as commissioner with the Cabildo. He later became the first democratically elected mayor of New Orleans.

When Pitot House was threatened with demolition in 1962, the Louisiana Landmarks Society rescued this historic home by moving it to its present location on Moss Street. It is now a museum.

## Old Spanish Customhouse
### 1300 Moss Street

Ten years before the founding of New Orleans, concessions were granted to Antoine Rivard de la Vigne and others in 1708. This site was the plantation of Jean François Huchet de Kernion from 1736 to 1771 and of Don Santiago Lorreins until 1807. It was after this date that the French colonial house was probably built or remodeled for Capt. Elie Beauregard by Robert Alexander, who built the first United States Customhouse on Canal Street between 1807 and 1809. The original Spanish Customhouse was demolished by Alexander at that time and he may have used its materials in the present house, resulting in its popular name, the Old Spanish Customhouse.

## Our Lady of the Rosary Rectory
*1342 Moss Street*

About 1834, Evariste Blanc had this Greek Revival mansion built on his Bayou St. John estate. His widow, Marie Fannie Labatut Blanc, planned to give the property to the Archdiocese of New Orleans for a parish church as early as 1855.

Fifty years later, in fulfillment of her mother's wishes, Sylvanie Blanc Denegre donated the family home for the establishment of Our Lady of the Rosary Parish. When a temporary church was built in 1907, the Blanc Mansion became the parish rectory, a function it has continued to fulfill ever since.

## Peristyle
*City Park*

A magnificent pavilion was built in City Park in 1906 and dedicated in 1908. It was originally known as the peristylium and is now called the peristyle.

Of Grecian style and architecture, it is encircled by majestic columns which foster the graceful, open-air effect of the sheltered platform. At night soft music, elegantly dressed dancers, and the moon's reflection on the lagoon waters all contributed to the fantasylike setting.

At the steps leading to the water's edge are two lions which were carved by Pietro Ghiloni.

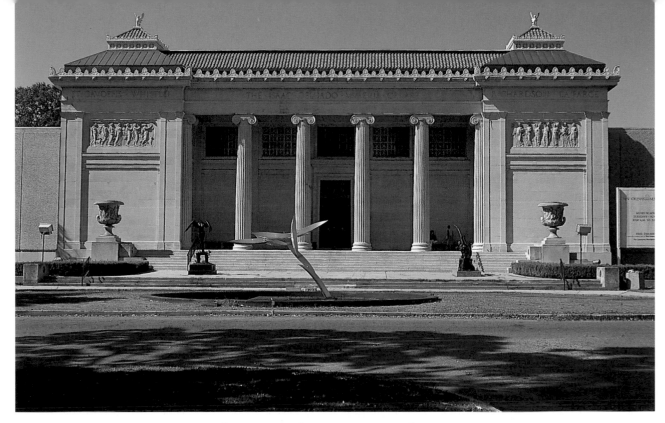

## The New Orleans Museum of Art
### City Park

Isaac Delgado, a successful sugar broker, left his native Jamaica in 1910 to seek his fortune in New Orleans. He donated funds to the city for the construction of the Isaac Delgado Museum of Art. Samuel A. Marx of Chicago designed the stately neoclassic beaux arts structure which opened on December 16, 1911.

In 1971 three wings were added to the original building, nearly tripling its size. It was then that the museum adopted its current name, recognizing a generous contribution from the city which helped make the expansion a reality.

The museum has become an invaluable cultural, educational, and recreational resource. It serves the city of New Orleans and the state of Louisiana with programs and exhibitions cultivating, promoting, and inspiring the knowledge, love, and appreciation of fine arts.

## McFadden House
### City Park

On the site of Allard Plantation, the original house was built in 1909 for Fred Bertrand.

Located just outside of the limits of City Park, the home was purchased ten years later by William McFadden. He completely rebuilt the house, which is now a forty-two-room mansion of brick and stucco with a red Spanish-tile roof.

McFadden sold the mansion to the City Park Board of Commissioners in 1942.

At the present time this stately showplace is leased to the Christian Brothers School.

## Florence A. Luling Mansion
### *1436 Leda Court*

This Italianate villa was built on three tracts of land in 1865 for Florence A. Luling, a wealthy New Orleans factor who had purchased the land in 1864.

The initial contract for the erection of Luling Mansion was with James Gallier, Sr., who executed the Palladio Italianate design after he had traveled extensively in Europe and Egypt. His untimely death in a boat explosion forced James Gallier, Jr., to finish the Luling project to settle his father's estate. The younger Gallier sought the advice and expertise of Richard Esterbrook, a noted and more experienced architect.

The Louisiana Jockey Club acquired the property on July 12, 1871.

The Luling Mansion is now owned by the Welcker family and is presently the residence of Clyde J. Welcker.

## Nicholas M. Benachi House
*2257 Bayou Road*

In 1859 this imposing mansion in the Greek Revival style was built for Nicholas M. Benachi, consul of Greece in New Orleans. Joseph and Peter Torre purchased the house in 1886. It was their family residence until it was bequeathed to the Louisiana Landmarks Society by Miss Venetia Torre and her brother, Louis J. Torre, in 1979. Robin and James G. Derbes bought it in 1981 with covenants for restoration and preservation.

## Cyprien Dufour House
*1705 Esplanade Avenue*

In 1859 this house was built for Cyprien Dufour, attorney-at-law and author of *Esquisses Locales*. The architects, Henry Howard and Albert Diettel, designed the mansion in the late Greek Revival and Italianate styles. Albert Baldwin, a prominent hardware merchant and banker, resided here from 1870 to 1912.

Note the impressive Doric columns, ironwork railings, and massive entablature.

## Edgar Germain Helaire Degas House
### *2306 Esplanade Avenue*

Degas, the French impressionist whose mother and grandmother were born in New Orleans, painted many famous subjects on a visit here in 1872-73 at the Esplanade Avenue home of Michel Musson, his uncle.

While visiting, Degas painted his acclaimed work of art, *The Cotton Market in New Orleans,* depicting his uncle's office. This painting is on display in the Municipal Museum in Pau, France. His *Portrait of Estelle* was bought by the Delgado Museum, now the New Orleans Museum of Art.

## John Gauché House
### *704 Esplanade Avenue*

Located on historic Esplanade Avenue, this striking Italianate villa was built in 1856 for John Gauché, who was an importer and dealer in crockery and chinaware. The land was part of the former city commons when it was purchased by Gauché from attorney Henry R. Denis. The house changed ownership several times and was restored twice, once in 1938 by Matilda Geddings Gray, who purchased it in 1937, and in 1969 by her niece, Matilda Gray Stream.

It is noted for its elaborate ironwork. Note the delicate iron railings and the iron lace which rims the entablature.

## Fisk-Hopkins House
### *730 Esplanade Avenue*

The original lot at 730 Esplanade Avenue was bought in 1860 by Edward Fisk, a bachelor who lived with his family at 740 Esplanade Avenue. The house included a library and billiard room for the gentlemen of the family.

Around 1871 the original one-story building and spacious garden land at 730 Esplanade were bought by Aristide Hopkins, agent of the Baroness de Pontalba. The Hopkins family resided in this building, adding a second level and cast-iron balcony supported by double braces of iron columns, until 1925 when it was sold to Mrs. Myrthe Celeste Stauffer Schwartz. This lovely home continues to be the residence of members of the Schwartz family.

## United States Mint
### *400 Esplanade Avenue*

The United States Branch Mint, a grand Greek Revival structure, was built in 1835. William Strickland was the architect and John Mitchell and Benjamin F. Fox were the builders. From 1856 to 1859 the building was renovated and fireproofed with Capt. Johnson K. Duncan supervising.

In 1861 the mint was seized by Confederate authorities and for a brief period Confederate coins were minted here. After New Orleans fell to Federal forces, William B. Mumford was hanged in front of the mint on June 7, 1862, for having torn down the United States flag. In 1909 the building ceased to be used as a mint. In 1932 it became a federal prison and until 1965 the United States Coast Guard was in occupancy.

The ownership of this magnificent structure was transferred to Louisiana in 1966. It was renovated from 1978 to 1980 as part of the Louisiana State Museum.

# The Steamboat Houses
*400 and 503 Egania Street*

At the end of Egania Street two unique mansions are located.

The house pictured here was built in 1875 for Milton P. Doullut, a riverboat pilot who came to New Orleans from France. Mr. Doullut evidently drew on his knowledge of riverboats as well as his creative imagination when building the house on the levee.

In 1912 the Doulluts' only child, Paul, built an identical house nearby.

Each home is surrounded by graceful, thin-columned galleries, draped with unusual strands of large wooden "pearls" and topped by an octagonal belvedere containing thirty-two tiny windows. Other features are reminiscent of those found on the ornate floating palaces that once traveled the Mississippi River.

The Steamboat Houses remain in the Doullut family today.

### The Chalmette Monument
*Chalmette National Historical Park*

In 1840 Gen. Andrew Jackson proposed this monument honoring the American victory over the British at the Battle of New Orleans in 1815 at Chalmette, a few miles downriver from the city.

Work began on the obelisk in 1856 and progressed slowly because of financial difficulties. It was completed in 1908 with help from the Daughters of the American Revolution, the U.S. Daughters of 1812, and the federal government.

### René Beauregard House Museum
*Chalmette National Historical Park*

This home was built in the 1830s and was later owned by Judge René Beauregard, the son of Gen. Pierre Gustave Toutant Beauregard. Judge Beauregard resided in the mansion with his family from 1880 to 1904.

The house is made of brick covered with cement and consists of two stories and an attic. Eight magnificent Doric columns support upper and lower galleries in the front and rear of the home. Remodelings of both the interior and the exterior, attributed to James Gallier, Jr., took place in 1856 and 1865.

In 1957 the structure was restored and is now the headquarters for the Chalmette National Historical Park.

## Our Lady of Guadalupe
## Mortuary Chapel
### *Rampart and Conti Streets*

The mortuary chapel of St. Anthony, now the church of Our Lady of Guadalupe, was closely associated with the history of the St. Louis Cemeteries in New Orleans. In 1826 the City Council forbade the holding of funeral services in St. Louis Cathedral since it was feared that the taking of corpses to the larger church was a means of spreading disease. The chapel was then constructed in 1826-27 by Gurlie and Guillot, architect-builders, to serve as a mortuary chapel.

It is a simple structure of plastered brick with an open, arched loggia surmounted by a belfry and steeple. This little church was dedicated on December 27, 1827, by the beloved Père Antoine and until 1860 was used solely for funerals.

## Jackson Square
### *Decatur and St. Peter Streets*

This historic square was laid out by Adrien de Pauger in March of 1721 according to the original city plan of Leblond de la Tour, engineer-in-chief of Louisiana. It was the French colonial Place d'Armes from 1721 to 1768, when Louisiana was transferred from France to Spain. It then became known as the Spanish colonial Plaza de Armas until November 30, 1803, when flag ceremonies were held symbolizing the return of Louisiana to France, and on December 20, 1803, from France to the United States.

Between 1850 and 1851 the square was transformed and renamed Jackson Square in honor of Maj. Gen. Andrew Jackson. Louis H. Pilié, city surveyor, designed the cast-iron fence and it was erected in 1851 by Pelanne Brothers of New Orleans.

*Reminiscent of Montmartre in Paris, France, artists now gather at Jackson Square to sell their paintings.*

*The impressive bronze statue in Jackson Square is of Maj. Gen. Andrew Jackson, who was the victorious hero of the Battle of New Orleans against the British in 1815.*

*Each morning brightly colored carriages, pulled by mules, get in line on the river side of Jackson Square in the Vieux Carré. Throughout the day the drivers take visitors on tours of the French Quarter, explaining the history of many points of interest.*

## Cathedral of St. Louis, King of France
*Jackson Square*

The St. Louis Cathedral, as it is popularly called, is the third church on this site. The first, designed by Adrien de Pauger, was erected in the 1720s and destroyed by the disastrous fire of 1788. The second, designed by Gilberto Guillemard, was dedicated as a cathedral on Christmas Eve 1794.

From 1849 to 1851 the second church was enlarged and redesigned by J. N. B. Pouilly, architects. In 1850 it was designated as the metropolitan church of the Archdiocese of New Orleans. This cathedral of magnificent, symmetric design became a minor basilica when Pope Paul VI bestowed this rank upon it in 1964.

*In the rear of St. Louis Basilica is St. Anthony's Garden, one of the most delightful places in the French Quarter. Oak, sycamore, and magnolia trees near the wall of the sanctuary make this small garden an intriguing sight.*

26

## Presbytère
*Jackson Square*

Designed in 1791 by architect Gilberto Guillemard, this important building was constructed through the generosity of Don Andrés Almonester y Roxas but building ceased in 1798 when he died. The building was finally completed in 1813 for the wardens of St. Louis Cathedral. It was then rented to the city by the Cathedral wardens for use as a courthouse and never was used as a rectory or presbytère. In 1853 it was sold to the city.

The rear wings were added in 1840 and the mansard roof was erected in 1847. In 1911 the historic structure was handed over to the Louisiana State Museum and renovated in 1962-63.

## Cabildo
*Jackson Square*

With construction financed and directed by Don Andrés Almonester y Roxas, this magnificent, monumental building was erected in the late 1790s by Don Gilberto Guillemard. The legislative assembly of the Spanish colonial government (the Illustrious Cabildo) held its sessions here from May 10, 1799, until November 30, 1803, when Louisiana was returned to France. On December 20, 1803, the documents were signed transferring the Louisiana Purchase Territory from France to the United States. From 1803 to 1853 the structure was the city hall of New Orleans and from 1853 to 1910 it housed the Supreme Court of Louisiana. The Cabildo has been the Louisiana State Museum since 1911.

The mansard roof and much of the building were damaged during a catastrophic fire in May 1988. Cypress is currently being primed for use in the restoration of this historic structure.

## Upper Pontalba Building
### *Jackson Square*

On the St. Peter side of Jackson Square stands the Upper Pontalba Building. It was designed by James Gallier, Sr., noted architect, and built by Samuel Stewart for Micaela Almonester, Baroness de Pontalba, who was the daughter of Don Andrés Almonester y Roxas. Construction was completed in 1850.

The Upper Pontalba and its twin, the Lower Pontalba, face each other across Jackson Square and are believed to be the first apartment buildings in America.

This structure is now owned by the city government.

## Lower Pontalba Building
### *Jackson Square*

The Lower Pontalba Building was erected for Micaela Almonester, Baroness de Pontalba, in 1850-51. It is directly across Jackson Square from its twin, the Upper Pontalba Building.

In 1927 William Ratcliffe Irby bequeathed this historic structure to the Louisiana State Museum.

## Rillieux-Waldhorn House
### 343 Royal Street

Rillieux-Waldhorn House was completed at the end of the eighteenth century for Vincent Rillieux, New Orleans merchant and great-grandfather of Edgar Degas, the noted French artist. The design of the house is attributed to Barthelemy Lafon.

The wrought-iron balconies of the building are notable examples of Spanish colonial craftsmanship.

The building is currently occupied by Waldhorn Company, Inc.

## Faulkner's House
### Pirate's Alley

In 1925 William Faulkner, Nobel laureate, wrote his first novel, *Soldier's Pay,* when he lived in the yellow house on Pirate's Alley, which runs between the Cabildo and the St. Louis Basilica. The building was erected in 1840 by the widow of John Baptiste LaBranche on this site, which was formerly part of the yard of a French colonial prison.

*A closeup view of the design used in the wrought-iron railing and brackets of Spanish colonial craftsmanship.*

## Manheim Galleries
### *409 Royal Street*

The building that now houses the Manheim Galleries was erected in 1821 as the Louisiana State Bank. It was designed by Benjamin Henry Boneval Latrobe, who also designed the south wing of the United States Capitol in Washington, D.C.

Latrobe died of yellow fever before construction was started and it was completed by Benjamin F. Fox.

## Banque de la Louisiane
### *417 Royal Street*

The building at 417 Royal Street was erected in 1795 by Vincent Rillieux. In 1805 it was purchased by the Banque de la Louisiane, the first bank established after the Louisiana Purchase. From 1841 to 1891 it was the residence of the Alonzo Morphy family, where Paul Morphy, the famous chess player, lived for nearly forty years. The building was given to Tulane University in 1920 by William Ratcliffe Irby.

It has been occupied by Brennan's Restaurant since 1955.

### Court of Two Sisters
*613 Royal Street*

This building dates back to 1832. It became known as the Court of Two Sisters between 1886 and 1916 when the two Camor sisters operated a popular variety store at this location. At the present time the noted restaurant occupies the historic structure.

### Cornstalk Hotel
*915 Royal Street*

In the early 1800s this interesting old home was the residence of Judge Francis Xavier Martin, first chief justice of the Louisiana Supreme Court.

A unique, intricate "cornstalk" cast-iron fence surrounds the house, which is now a lovely hotel in the Victorian tradition of elegance.

## Gallier House Museum
### 1118-32 Royal Street

James Gallier, Jr., one of New Orleans' most noted and innovative architects, designed this elegant, Victorian *Vieux Carré* house. He had it built in 1857 as his private residence. This opulent home and its furnishings reflect the taste and lifestyle of mid-nineteenth century New Orleans.

## Miltenberger Home
### Royal and Dumaine Streets

The Miltenberger Home is at the corner of Royal and Dumaine streets. It was built in 1839 by the widow of Dr. Christian Miltenberger, who was a surgeon at the Battle of New Orleans.

*The design is oak leaf and acorn on the galleries of the Miltenberger Home.*

## LaBranche Building
### *Royal and St. Peter Streets*

The LaBranche Building was erected by Jean Baptiste LaBranche, a wealthy sugar planter, around 1835. The cast-iron galleries, in the oak leaf and acorn design, were added after 1850.

## Madame John's Legacy
### *632 Dumaine Street*

Madame John's Legacy, one of the oldest houses in New Orleans, was built in 1788 by an American builder, Robert Jones, for a Spanish officer, Don Manuel Lanzos, whose former house was destroyed by fire. Some of the materials from the original house were used in the present French colonial-style home, which is of *briquette-entre-poteaux* (brick between posts) construction over a raised brick basement.

George Washington Cable, the famous New Orleans writer, gave the house its popular name, Madame John's Legacy, when he used the building as the setting of his story, "'Tite Poulette." In 1925 this quaint, unique house was bought by Mrs. I. I. Lemann, who donated it to the Louisiana State Museum in 1947.

## Shotgun Row
### *Vieux Carré*

In various parts of the city one finds "shotgun" style houses such as these that were built in a row. Usually there are four or five rooms, each leading into another in a straight line. On occasion one finds a hallway on one side of the rooms. On the side of each house is an alleyway giving access to a small backyard.

## Pierre Maspero's Slave Exchange
### 440 Chartres Street

The Slave Exchange was established at 440 Chartres Street in 1788 and within this structure slaves were sold.

It is said that in this building Gen. Andrew Jackson met with the Lafitte brothers and planned the defense for the Battle of New Orleans.

*This is a view looking down Chartres Street toward the Cathedral.*

*Looking down upon the rooftops of Chartres Street is fascinating.*

## Napoleon House
### *500 Chartres Street*

Napoleon House, built prior to 1798, was the residence of New Orleans Mayor Nicholas Girod. It was here that plans were made to help Napoleon escape from St. Helena. If the rescue had been successful, this home was to be at his disposal.

## Old Spanish Arsenal
### *615 St. Peter Street*

The Old Spanish Arsenal, 615 St. Peter Street, occupies the site of the old Spanish prison, which was built in 1769. The Arsenal was erected in 1839 during Gov. A. B. Roman's administration and converted into a museum in 1915.

*The ponderous iron door to the Old Spanish Arsenal seems appropriately ominous.*

## Lafitte's Blacksmith Shop
*941 Bourbon Street*

For generations this quaint eighteenth-century cottage, located in the *Vieux Carré,* has been called Lafitte's Blacksmith Shop. It is commonly believed that Jean Lafitte and his brother, Pierre, used it to conceal their smuggling operations, although no historical confirmation connects it with the infamous pirates. A Monsieur Duroche was the original owner and it remained in his family for seventy years.

*Briquette-entre-poteaux* was the construction used by many builders in Louisiana well into the nineteenth century.

## LeCarpentier-Beauregard-Keyes
## House
### *1113 Chartres Street*

This house with its carved entablature and pediment, majestic columns and pilasters, was erected in 1826 by François Correjolles, architect, and James Lambert, builder. The original owner was Joseph LeCarpentier, auctioneer and grandfather of chess champion Paul Morphy.

The adjacent walled garden was built by John A. Merle, who bought the property in 1839. From 1866 to 1868 it was the home of Gen. P. G. T. Beauregard, C.S.A. The house and garden were restored in the late 1940s by the novelist Frances Parkinson Keyes, who lived here until her death in 1970.

The Keyes Foundation maintains the house, which is open to the public.

## Old Ursuline Convent
### 1102 Chartres Street

The existing Ursuline Convent, constructed of brick covered with stucco, was completed in 1752. The architect was Ignace François Broutin and the builder was Claude Joseph Villars Dubreuil. It replaced the original convent built in 1727-34 near the same site. It was occupied until 1824 by the Ursuline nuns, who opened a hospital and orphanage and who were charitable to the people of New Orleans. Then it became the residence of the bishops and archbishops of New Orleans from 1824 until 1899.

The Archdiocese of New Orleans restored the stately old building in the 1970s for use as its archival repository and it was renamed Archbishop Antoine Blanc Memorial.

*This is a closeup view of the balcony above the convent's entrance portico.*

## French Market
*Decatur Street*

While New Orleans was under Spanish rule, the French Market on Decatur Street was erected in 1791. In 1812 the market was destroyed by a hurricane but was rebuilt in 1813. It was completely modernized in 1937-38. The market extends for several city blocks and any type of food can be bought here – fish, meat, fruits, and vegetables.

At one end of the market is the Café du Monde, a street-side cafe where one can drink *café noir* (black coffee) or *café au lait* (coffee with milk) and enjoy *beignets* (small, crisp doughnuts sprinkled with confectioners' sugar) at all hours.

*Farmers bring fresh produce to the market at dawn.*

*Small shops are found on the side of the market.*

41

## Arnaud's Restaurant
### *813 Bienville Street*

Arnaud's Restaurant was established in 1918 by Arnaud Cazenave, from France. He was affectionately called "Count Arnaud." In front of the restaurant, the lights span the length of the block.

In 1978 Archie Casbarian bought the restaurant from Germaine Cazenave Wells, Count Arnaud's daughter.

## Gardette-LePretre House
### *716 Dauphine Street*

In 1836 Joseph Coulon Gardette commissioned Frederic Roy to build this house. Jean Baptiste LePretre, a planter, purchased it in 1839 and lived there until 1878. During his residency he added the cast-iron galleries.

On June 2, 1861, part of the captured flagstaff of Fort Sumter was presented to the Orleans Guards at this house. The flagstaff had been sent by Gen. P. G. T. Beauregard, C.S.A.

## Antoine's Restaurant
### 713 St. Louis Street

One of America's most historic restaurants was established by Antoine Alciatore, who came to New Orleans in 1840 from Marseilles, France. Jules Alciatore, Antoine's son, took over the management of the establishment after his father's death. Today it is operated by Roy Alciatore, a grandson, in the same conscientious manner as always.

## Hermann-Grima House
### 820 St. Louis Street

Samuel Hermann assigned the construction of this house to William Brand, architect-builder, in 1831. In 1844 it was purchased by Felix Grima, judge, attorney, and notary public, whose family kept ownership until 1921. The Christian Woman's Exchange acquired the house in 1924 and opened it to the public as a house museum. It is important as an example of the American influence on New Orleans architecture.

## Court of the Three Arches
### 633 Toulouse Street

Designed by Benjamin F. Fox, this house was built for Dr. Germain Ducatel in 1825. The balcony railings are crafted of cypress instead of the iron so popular at that time.

*The three arched doorways leading into the flagstone-paved patio account for the name "Court of the Three Arches."*

## Dolliole House
### 933 St. Philip Street

This quaint, Creole cottage was built in 1805 by Jean Louis Dolliole, a free man of color who lived here until approximately 1830.

Dolliole also built several houses in the Marigny and Tremé faubourgs, as well as in the *Vieux Carré.*

The cottage changed hands until it was abandoned in 1952 to the elements of nature for twenty-eight years. The picturesque home completely deteriorated.

It was purchased by Ann and Frank Masson in 1980, and Mr. Masson, an architect, directed the authentic restoration.

Note the sloping roof and the batten blinds which lend a closed and secret appearance to the now-loved home.

## Old Spanish Stables
### *716-24 Governor Nicholls Street*

The Old Spanish Stables were built as commercial livery stables in 1834 for Judge Gallien Preval. Though they are commonly called the Spanish Cavalry Stables and Barracks, the Spanish soldiers had left the city many years before the stables were erected.

A beautiful house now stands on this historic site.

*Today a bright, verdant patio has replaced the old stables.*

## Jean Baptiste Thierry House
### *721 Governor Nicholls Street*

Constructed in 1814, this house is one of the oldest examples of Greek Revival architecture in New Orleans. Designing the building for Jean Baptiste Thierry, editor of *Le Courrier de la Louisiane*, the original architects were Arsene Lacarriere Latour and Henry S. Latrobe. Architect Richard Koch restored the house in 1940.

## Sauvinet-Lewis-Baus House
### *831 Governor Nicholls Street*

Joseph Sauvinet and his wife, the original owners, built this house in 1822. They had purchased the land from Bartholome Bosque in 1803. A small cottage was added later by Dr. George W. Lewis, grandson of the Sauvinets, who used it for an office.

This lovely home has been completely restored. The floors are made of cypress, and there are two back-to-back fireplaces on each floor — both utilizing the same chimney. The two-story house is brick, covered with a layer of stucco. A wooden gallery spans the second floor.

The courtyards of the house are included in the Spring Fiesta Tour because of their serene beauty.

Mr. and Mrs. John V. Baus, who bought the home in 1973, maintain it as their private residence.

## United States Customhouse
### *423 Canal Street*

Located on Canal Street, four blocks from the Mississippi River, the United States Customhouse in New Orleans was built on a full city square. Constructed of Quincy, Massachusetts granite with brick backing, approximately four feet thick, it was designed by A. T. Wood, architect.

Construction began in 1848 but was halted in 1861 because of the Civil War. Work on the massive building resumed in 1871 and the present third story was completed in 1881. A fourth story was originally planned but never built. The architecture of this historic structure is modified Egyptian.

Pictured is the Great Marble Hall, which the designer labeled "The General Business Room." It measures 95 feet by 125 feet and is 54 feet high. The floor is laid in squares of white marble with black marble borders. The ceiling is formed by a skylight, framed in iron, wood, and glass, and is supported by fourteen white, Italian marble Corinthian columns, forty-one feet high and four feet in diameter. Each column has a carved head of Mercury, Roman god of commerce, and moon goddess Luna, for the Crescent City.

*The marble was shipped into this country in crude blocks and the pillars, bases, and capitals of the magnificent columns were fashioned by stonecutters in Boston, Massachusetts.*

# Riverfront Streetcar

The fascinating ''Red Streetcar'' went into operation on August 14, 1988. It runs along the riverfront from Stop #1, Esplanade Avenue, upriver to Stop #10, Robin Street. Each stop offers something of interest.

Stop #2 — The French Market Farmers' Market.

Stop #3 — The French Market and Decatur Street merchants.

Stop #4 — Jackson Square, St. Louis Cathedral, the Cabildo, the Presbytère, and the Steamboat *Natchez*.

Stop #5 — Woldenberg Riverfront Park and the Aquarium of the Americas.

Stop #6 — The Aquarium of the Americas and the Canal Street Ferry.

Stop #7 — The paddlewheeler *Creole Queen* and the Poydras Street entrance to Riverwalk.

Stop #8 — The Julia Street entrance to Riverwalk and the New Orleans Convention Center.

Stop #9 — The historic Warehouse District.

*Sightseeing ships docked at Canal Street are a familiar sight along the riverfront.*

*The huge, fascinating, recently built Aquarium of the Americas on Canal Street at the riverfront.*

*View of buildings along the Mississippi River at Canal Street.*

*The bustling Canal Street dock at the site of the aquarium.*

## Steamboat *Natchez*
### *Woldenberg Park*

The steam sternwheeler *Natchez* is the ninth steamer to be named after the Indian tribe native to southern Mississippi. It was launched April 3, 1975, at Braithwaite, Louisiana, twelve miles below New Orleans.

The *Natchez* is modeled after the packet boat *Hudson*, which plied the Mississippi River in 1886 until 1905 from Pittsburgh to Cincinnati. The indestructible steam engines from old ships were commonly transferred to new ships. Such is the case with the *Natchez*. Her engines and other engine room machinery were supplied by the United States Steel Corporation from their towboat *Clairton* (1927-65), which pushed steel and coal from Pittsburgh to New Orleans.

Today, aboard the *Natchez* one can enjoy daytime cruises, evening cruises (with or without dinner), and moonlight dance cruises on Saturday nights.

The *Natchez's* steam calliope is played for three hours each day and the happy sound blends beautifully with the voice of the Mississippi River.

## Gallier Hall
### *545 St. Charles Avenue*

Gallier Hall, a magnificent Greek Revival building, was designed by James Gallier, Sr., and erected in 1845-53. It was the New Orleans City Hall until 1957. In this building Federal forces from Capt. David G. Farragut's fleet declared possession of the city on April 29, 1862. Jefferson Davis, president of the Confederate States of America, Gen. P. G. T. Beauregard, C.S.A., Mayor Martin Behrman, Mayor de Lesseps S. Morrison, and other notables have lain in state in the hall's parlor.

## Robert E. Lee Monument
### *St. Charles Avenue*

Confederate general Robert E. Lee's monument stands commandingly at Lee Circle on St. Charles Avenue.

*The pediment bas-relief was sculpted by Robert A. Launitz.*

51

## Howard Memorial Library
### *615 Howard Avenue*

Henry Hobson Richardson, Louisiana-born architect, died in 1886. This historically important structure bears the mark of his architectural style, which became known as Richardsonian Romanesque. It was built in 1888-89 for Mrs. Annie Howard Parrott as a memorial to her father, Charles T. Howard. The Howard Library joined the Tilton Library on Tulane University's campus in 1941.

The building was used during World War II for British war relief activities. On January 1, 1945, a disastrous fire destroyed much of the interior and part of the roof.

In 1989 the property was purchased by Patrick F. Taylor, a well-known New Orleans petroleum engineer and philanthropist. The building is currently undergoing a complete restoration of the interior as well as the exterior.

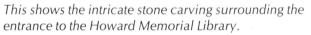

*This shows the intricate stone carving surrounding the entrance to the Howard Memorial Library.*

*Detail of stone carving.*

## Confederate Museum
### 929 Camp Street

Louisiana's oldest museum is Confederate Memorial Hall, which was dedicated on January 8, 1891. Thomas Sully designed the massive structure to harmonize with the adjoining building, the Howard Memorial Library. The museum was built as a repository for records and memorabilia of the Civil War by Frank T. Howard. He donated it to the Louisiana Historical Association as a memorial to Charles T. Howard, his father.

Jefferson Davis died in New Orleans and lay in state in Memorial Hall on May 29, 1893.

The building continues to be operated as a museum by the Louisiana Historical Association, which was founded on April 11, 1889.

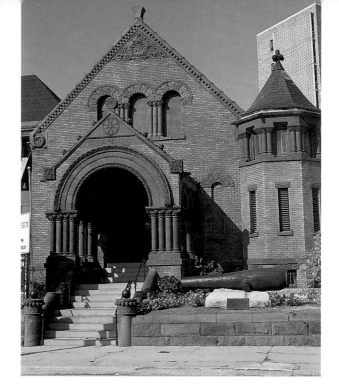

## Thomas P. Leathers House
### 2027 Carondelet Street

In 1859 this residence was erected for Capt. Thomas P. Leathers. During his fifty-seven-year career he built and commanded seven steamboats called *Natchez*, including the famed ship which raced the *Robert E. Lee* in 1870. At the age of eighty, he died here on June 13, 1896.

This magnificent home was designed by Henry Thiberge for William K. Day.

In 1900 it became the home of Dr. E. W. Jones. Later occupants included other members of the Jones family as well as the Charles F. Buck, Jr., family and the George J. Mayer family.

## Loeber House
### *1629 Coliseum Street*

At the corner of Euterpe and Coliseum streets stands a spendid, turreted Victorian mansion. Dr. Frederick Loeber, a distinguished doctor, resided here at one time. For many years he was chief surgeon at Touro Infirmary.

The house has fallen into disrepair and is now being restored by its owners, Maxine and John De Lay.

## Henry Morton Stanley House
### *1729 Coliseum Street*

This house was originally built in the early 1800s at 904 Orange Street for William Goodrich, a partner in the New Orleans jewelry firm of Hyde and Goodrich. In 1981 it was moved to 1729 Coliseum Street and restored.

Henry Hope Stanley, a British-born cotton merchant, purchased the Orange Street property in 1858. He befriended a young Welsh runaway cabin boy and took him home, named him Henry Morton Stanley, and reared him as his son. Young Stanley joined the Confederate Army at the beginning of the Civil War. After he had been taken prisoner and released, he made his way to New York, where he became a journalist. The newspaper sent him to Africa to search for Dr. David Livingston. Upon finding the doctor, he greeted him with the famous question, ''Dr. Livingston, I presume?'' He earned a knighthood for other African explorations which followed.

## William Henry Clay King House
### *1539 Camp Place*

Built about 1883 for Mrs. William Henry Clay King, this historic old home changed hands several times. It was then abandoned for approximately forty years until 1969, when Margaret and Blaise D'Antoni purchased the property. At that time complete restoration took place. The present owners and residents are Mr. and Mrs. Philip Johnson.

*An example of the beautifully carved cypress brackets and railings used in the William Henry Clay King House.*

### Archibald Bouleware House
*1531 Camp Place*

In 1854 this stately brick house was built for Archibald Bouleware. The residence was purchased in 1880 by William H. Bofinger, president of the American District Telephone Company and president of the National Automatic Fire Alarm Company of Louisiana.

Popular in the nineteenth century, the arched iron trellis in front of the house is an unusual surviving example of garden ornamentation.

### François Adolphe D'Aquin House
*2333 Camp Street*

In 1852 this residence was built for François Adolphe D'Aquin. In 1904 it was the home of the widow of Joseph A. Shakespeare, mayor of New Orleans from 1888 to 1892. The present owners, Ernest and Clare Beals, purchased and restored the property in 1963.

Noted for its handsome leaded-glass door and the 300-year-old registered oak tree which stands in front of the house, it was on the Spring Fiesta agenda in 1965.

## Henry Sullivan Buckner House
## Soulé College
*1410 Jackson Avenue*

This notable Garden District mansion in the Greek Revival style was erected in 1856 for Henry Sullivan Buckner. Buckner's daughter and her husband, Cartwright Eustis, were the residents. It was occupied by Soulé College from 1923 to 1983.

*This view of the Buckner House shows the spectacular ironwork gate and railing.*

## Lavinia C. Dabney House
*2265 St. Charles Avenue*

Lavinia C. Dabney engaged Gallier, Turpin, and Company to build this Garden District mansion in 1856-57. It was the residence of the Jonas O. Rosenthal family from 1893 to 1952. From 1952 to 1972 it was occupied as the diocesan house of the Episcopal Diocese of Louisiana.

## Jacob U. Payne House
*1134 First Street*

This exceptional example of mid-nineteenth-century New Orleans suburban architecture was built at the end of the 1840s for Jacob U. Payne. Its wide galleries, with Ionic columns on the ground floor and columns with Tower of the Winds capitals on the second floor, span the width of the house. It remained in the Payne family until its sale in 1935.

The present owners are Mr. and Mrs. Frank Strachan.

The house's claim to fame as the place of death of Jefferson Davis, a close friend of Payne's son-in-law, Judge Charles Erasmus Fenner, is told on a granite marker erected by the Ladies' Confederate Memorial Association in 1930.

*Note the precise carving of the columns, entablature, and doorway of this stately home.*

### Jamison-Carroll House
*1315 First Street*

Designed and built in 1869 by Samuel Jamison, this spectacular mansion has many elaborate Italianate features. Joseph Carroll, a Virginian who became one of the most successful cotton factors in the city, was its first owner.

The present owners are Dr. and Mrs. Morton Brown.

## Albert Hamilton Brevard House
### *1239 First Street*

In 1857 this imposing Greek Revival house was built for Albert Hamilton Brevard by James H. Calrow and Charles Pride. In 1869 the house was bought by Emory Clapp, who added a library wing. It was the Clapp family residence until 1935. Since then ownership of the house has changed several times.

## William H. McClellan House
### *1006 Washington Avenue*

From 1868 to 1869 this splendid mansion was built for William H. McClellan, owner of a ship supply business.

The impressive columns surrounding the first-story gallery are Ionic and the columns surrounding the second-story gallery are Corinthian. This design indicates the Greek Revival influence. However, the bracketed eaves and the segmented, arched windows are Italianate in style.

## Alexander Harris House
### *2127 Prytania Street*

On shady, tree-lined Prytania Street in uptown New Orleans stands this classic Greek Revival, raised villa which was originally built in 1857-58 by Alexander Harris, a cotton factor. It was designed by T. K. Wharton, whose diary, now preserved in the New York Public Library, noted that this house "promises to be the handsomest piece of work in the district." It was purchased in 1871 by John H. Maginnis and eventually given to the Red Cross. In 1954 the lovely home was bought and restored by Dr. and Mrs. Clyde Crassons.

## Toby's Corner
### *2340 Prytania Street*

Believed to be the oldest house in the Garden District of New Orleans, Toby House was built at the edge of the old Livaudais Plantation in 1838 for Thomas Toby. It is located at the corner of First and Prytania streets, hence the name, "Toby's Corner."

Toby was a Philadelphia businessman who came to this city in the early 1800s and made a fortune as a wheelwright. After Toby's death, the house was sold in 1858 to the Westfeldt family, whose descendants are still in residence.

Broad galleries surround the house, which is raised on brick piers. This type of architecture reflects the style of the West Indies plantation homes built at that time.

*From the first-story entrance to the Toby House, one can see the lush greenery of the garden.*

### Bradish-Johnson House
### Louise S. McGehee School
*2343 Prytania Street*

Built in 1872 for the prominent Louisiana sugar planter Bradish Johnson, this mansion's design is attributed to architect James Freret. It reflects the influence of the French Ecole des Beaux Arts, where Freret studied in the early 1860s. From 1892 to 1929 it was the residence of Walter Denegre and has been occupied by the Louise S. McGehee School since 1929.

*A detail of the rounded end of the upper gallery.*

### Walter Grinnan Robinson House
*1415 Third Street*

One of the largest and most elegant mansions in the Garden District was built for Walter Grinnan Robinson in the late 1850s. Robinson came from Virginia to live in New Orleans.

The upper and lower galleries feature decorative rounded ends, a design often used by James Gallier, Sr., and James Gallier, Jr. Four majestic columns and two pilasters were used on each gallery. The massive entablature has an ornamental pediment.

## Col. Robert H. Short Villa
## Favrot House
### 1448 Fourth Street

Colonel Short's villa, now the Favrot House, was built in 1859 for Col. Robert H. Short of Kentucky. Henry Howard was the architect and Robert Huyhe was the builder.

On September 1, 1863, the Federal forces occupying the city seized the house as property of an absent rebel.

In March, 1864, the house briefly served as the executive mansion of the newly elected governor of Louisiana, Michael Hahn. It then became the residence of Maj. Gen. Nathaniel P. Banks, U.S. Commander, Department of the Gulf.

The house was returned to Colonel Short by the United States government on August 15, 1865, and he lived in it until his death in 1890.

An addition was made in 1906 and the house was restored in 1950.

The unusual cast-iron morning glory and cornstalk fence was furnished by the Philadelphia Foundry of Wood and Perot.

The present owners are Mr. and Mrs. Thomas B. Favrot.

## Alfred Grima House
### 1604 Fourth Street

The Alfred Grima House was built about 1857 by Cornelius Bickwell Payne. In 1861 it sold to Thomas L. Clarke. Alfred Grima acquired the mansion from Clarke in 1890 and had it completely remodeled within a year by Paul Andry and John McNally.

In 1925, the lovely formal garden at the side of the house was completed by Charles R. Armstrong. The garden trellis was built in 1926 and was the last work of architect Samuel S. Labouisse.

In 1981 Clarisse Claiborne Grima, widow of Alfred Grima, Jr., donated the house to the Historic New Orleans Collection upon her death.

This magnificent home was acquired by private ownership in 1987.

## Orleans Club
*5005 St. Charles Avenue*

The Orleans Club, 5005 St. Charles Avenue, was built in 1868. This is an impressive three-story building with delicate iron filigree trimming the two galleries which span the width of the house. The three gables at the third-floor level have graceful, arched pediments and iron balcony railings.

In 1925 it was purchased and remodeled by the exclusive New Orleans Women's Club.

## Marks Isaacs Mansion
### *5120 St. Charles Avenue*

Set in an entire city block, this opulent mansion was built in 1907 by Mr. and Mrs. Marks Isaacs, owners of one of the major Canal Street department stores at that time. Neo-Italianate in style, it has an overhanging roof, broad galleries embellished with intricate iron railings, paired columns, and ornamental corner pillars.

When Mrs. Isaacs died, the house sold to Frank B. Williams, a prominent lumberman. It became the residence of his son, Harry P. Williams, an aviation pioneer, and his wife, Marguerite Clark, the silent-screen star. Williams died in an airplane crash in 1936 and Mrs. Williams sold the home to Robert S. Eddy in 1940, when she moved to New York.

After Mrs. Eddy died, the mansion was sold to Mr. and Mrs. Harry Latter. They donated it to the New Orleans Public Library as a memorial to their son, Milton H. Latter, who had been killed in Okinawa during World War II.

## St. Charles Avenue Streetcar

The St. Charles Avenue line is the last original streetcar line still in use in the city. The first electric streetcar was introduced in 1893.

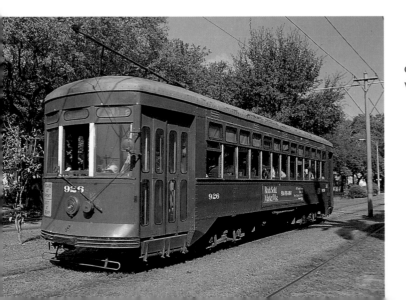

## Joseph Fonaris House
### *2115 Palmer Avenue*

Built in 1897 for Joseph Fonaris, this unusual house has a three-story octagonal tower surfaced with patterned wooden shingles, a practice in vogue on frame houses in the 1890s.

## Greenville Hall
## Loyola University
### *7214 St. Charles Avenue*

Greenville Hall is an exceptional Italianate structure designed by William Fitzner. It was built in 1882 for St. Mary's Academy, a girls' school established in 1861 by Dominican nuns from Cabra, Ireland. The sisters acquired the present land in 1864, when it was located in the small picturesque village of Greenville. New Orleans annexed the community in 1870 and in 1910 the academy became St. Mary's Dominican College.

The building is noted for its broad, upper and lower galleries, symmetrical arches between gallery posts, and unique cupola.

In the 1980s the Jesuits of Loyola University purchased the Dominican campus. Greenville Hall was among the buildings annexed and renovated.

*A tranquil shrine on the grounds of Loyola University's Broadway Campus.*

### Gibson Hall
### Tulane University
*6823 St. Charles Avenue*

Gibson Hall was constructed in 1893-94. The design of the building by the architectural firm of Harrod and Andry won a national competition and the firm was then engaged to design the rest of the original campus.

The university was founded in 1834 as the Medical College of Louisiana and later became the state-chartered University of Louisiana. The university accepted several gifts from Paul Tulane and in 1884 it was recognized as the Tulane University of Louisiana. That year the state dropped its charter and Tulane University became a private institution.

Substantial gifts were also given to the university by Josephine Louise Newcomb in memory of her daughter.

### Jefferson Parish Courthouse
*719 South Carrollton Avenue*

The construction of this stately Greek Revival building was completed in 1855. It was designed by Henry Howard, a well-known architect, and built by Robert Crozier and Frederick Wing. Until 1874, when Carrollton was annexed by New Orleans, it served as the Jefferson Parish Courthouse. The building became McDonogh School #23 in 1879 and later became Benjamin Franklin Senior High School in 1957.

The magnificent structure is now being restored.

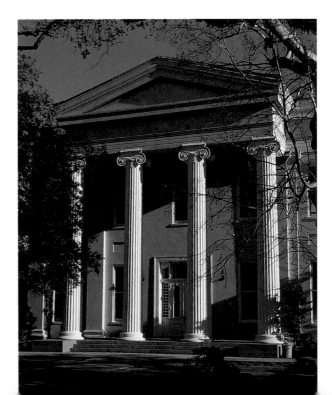

## Van Benthuysen-Elms Mansion
### *3029 St. Charles Avenue*

Attributed to architect Lewis E. Reynolds, the mansion was built in 1869 for "Yankee in Grey," Capt. Watson Van Benthuysen II, C.S.A. He was a relative by marriage of Jefferson Davis and quartermaster of the presidential convoy that fled Richmond in April 1865.

Captain Van Benthuysen became a merchant and industrialist. Born in New York in 1833, he died here in 1901.

The house served as German Consulate 1931-41. It became John Elms' family residence in 1951.

*This small, lovely garden was the first garden at Longue Vue to be developed in the 1920s by Mr. and Mrs. Edgar Stern. It was their favorite garden.*

# Courtyards and Patios

In New Orleans, a city of contrasts, many of the courtyards and patios in the *Vieux Carré* are hidden from view by old brick walls and buildings. Occasionally one can see through the grill of an iron gate and enjoy the secret loveliness of the colorful flowers and greenery flourishing in these private places.

The French colonists called their hidden gardens *cours* and the Spanish called them *patios*. Many of the tropical flowers and plants which thrive in this damp, humid climate were shipped from the West Indies and the Orient.

Some of the larger courtyards, such as the Court of Two Sisters and Princess Heine's Courtyard, have become successful restaurants. It is, indeed, delightful to have dinner under the stars with soft candlelight and music adding to the enchanting ambiance.

In 1722, when Leblond de la Tour drew the plans of the colony, it consisted of just the unique *Vieux Carré,* which is bounded by Canal Street, Esplanade Avenue, North Rampart Street, and the Mississippi River. As New Orleans grew, this became the central section of the city.

## Longue Vue Gardens
### *7 Bamboo Road*

There are twenty-three fountains throughout the gardens at Longue Vue. The sight and sound of these fountains create a refreshing feeling of serenity. The most impressive is the fountain in the Spanish Court, with its reflecting pool and its graceful, arching jets. Around the circular part of the pool one sees potted plants in bloom according to the season.

*In the Yellow Garden one finds a profusion of yellow blooms. Climbing the columns of the loggia is Carolina Yellow Jessamine.*

The contemporary fountain in the northeast corner of the lawn is delicately engineered and balanced to create the motion of swimming and flying. It was designed by Lin Emery of New Orleans and is entitled Arabesque.

This beautifully landscaped garden of azaleas and camellias has a captivating canal running through it.

Clipped boxwood hedges form a miniature parterre from which to view the Spanish Court.

## François Seignouret House and Patio
### *520 Royal Street*

The house was built in 1816 by François Seignouret, a native of Bordeaux, France, and a veteran of the Battle of New Orleans. A rear wing was added in 1822 by architect and builder Robert Brand. Pierre Brulatour bought the house in 1870 and conducted a wine importing business here until 1887. The building was restored in 1918 by William R. Irby as his residence.

In 1948 WDSU-TV became the first television station in New Orleans and opened its offices here in 1949.

The well-kept patio is paved with flagstones, and potted plants surround the fountain. It is popularly known as the Brulatour Patio.

*The timeworn stairs at the Brulatour Patio are made of cypress.*

74

## Jean François Merieult House
*533 Royal Street*

On the site of the first barracks, forges, and workshops of the Company of the Indies, this house was erected for Jean François Merieult in 1792. The disastrous fire of 1794 destroyed every building in the area except this structure. Manuel J. de Lizardi remodeled it in 1832 in the contemporary style of that day. In 1938 further restoration was directed by Richard Koch, architect, for the building's owners, Gen. and Mrs. L. Kemper Williams.

The Merieult House has been open to the public since 1966 as the home of the Historic New Orleans Collection of the Kemper and Leila Williams Foundation.

The photograph shows the courtyard at the rear of the Merieult House.

## Patio
### *718 Toulouse Street*

This lovely patio can be seen through an iron gate at 718 Toulouse Street. It is part of the museum complex of the Historic New Orleans Collection. Note the lacy ironwork framing the galleries, and the intricate pattern of the brick paving.

## 1850 House Courtyard
### *523 St. Ann Street*

The 1850 House courtyard is fascinating with its timeworn flagstone flooring, its view of the batten blinds on the windows and doors of the 1850 House, and its lush green plants.

*A view of the slave quarters at the 1850 House in the Lower Pontalba Building on Jackson Square.*

## Hotel Maison de Ville
### 727 Toulouse Street

In the heart of the *Vieux Carré* stands the fascinating Hotel Maison de Ville. Built in 1743 by Monsieur Peychaud, it has been perfectly preserved since the days when most of eastern North America was still a British colony and New Orleans was under French rule.

*Closeup view of the courtyard fountain.*

*Both the soft sound of the fountain and the sight of the greenery in the courtyard at Maison de Ville create an atmosphere of peace and serenity.*

# Audubon Cottages
## *509 Dauphine Street*

Owned by Hotel Maison de Ville and located nearby are the Audubon Cottages. They cannot be seen from the street. However, inside the locked gate are several small cottages which were built in 1788 and have been completely restored.

Each cottage has a separate, fenced-in courtyard with an iron gate leading into the central pool area.

The noted American naturalist, John James Audubon, his wife, and two sons lived here. Audubon created many of his wildlife masterpieces and oil portraits, as well as tutored neighborhood children, while in residence here.

*Another view of the central pool area.*

## Chateau LeMoyne Patio
### *301 Dauphine Street*

The Chateau LeMoyne, a beautifully appointed small hotel, is located in the *Vieux Carré* at 301 Dauphine Street. It was named after Jean Baptiste LeMoyne, Sieur de Bienville, who founded the city of New Orleans in 1718. Part of the hotel was built in 1971 and combined with the perfectly restored original buildings and slave quarters which had been designed by James Gallier, Sr., in 1847.

There are several patios at the Chateau LeMoyne Hotel. This one shows a view of the restored slave quarters.

*This patio is paved with old brick around an attractive fountain.*

## Daniel Clark Patio
### *823 Royal Street*

This is the patio of the home where Daniel Clark, an Irishman, lived. He shot Governor Claiborne in the leg during a duel. It is said that Clark was one of Jean Lafitte's secret agents.

## Marchand House
### *830 Royal Street*

The quaint, graceful, winding stairway gives access to the living quarters at 830 Royal Street. The cypress stairway is highly admired by visitors.

Built in 1808 by Solomon Prevost, the house was later sold to Jean Baptiste Marchand.

## Nine-O-Five Royal Hotel
### *905 Royal Street*

The red tulips and white cast-iron furniture in this patio at the side of a small hotel, at 905 Royal Street, attract attention.

## Princess of Monaco Courtyard
*912 Royal Street*

New Orleans was known from the earliest days for its beautiful and talented women. One of the first was Alice Heine, the first American princess of Monaco.

She was born in 1858 at 912 Royal Street, one of the famous Miltenberger houses, to Marie Celeste Miltenberger and Michael Heine, a German banker.

In 1874 Alice's father took her to Paris to choose a husband and one year later she married the duc de Richelieu and became the duchess of Richelieu. After just four happy years the duc de Richelieu died and left Alice the title, the chateau, the house in Paris, and fifteen million dollars.

Ten years later Alice married the first Prince Albert of Monaco and became princess of Monaco. The marriage was not happy. They separated in 1902 and were eventually divorced.

Her marriages, the divorce from the prince, and later romances in Europe were followed closely in New Orleans newspapers at the turn of the century.

## Hermann-Grima House Courtyard
*820 St. Louis Street*

The courtyard is at the rear of the Hermann-Grima House. In this view one sees the slave quarters and the kitchen. Once a week several ladies in antebellum-period costumes come to the house to cook Creole food. Note the batten blinds on the doors giving access to the courtyard.

82

## Dolliole House Garden
*933 St. Philip Street*

The peach tree adds to the beauty of the colorful blooms in the garden at the rear of Dolliole House.

*View of the Dolliole House garden from the kitchen door.*

### Court of Two Sisters Courtyard
*613 Royal Street*

In the rear of the Court of Two Sisters is a lovely courtyard which is hidden from the passerby.

### Old Spanish Courtyard
*532-34 Madison Street*

Visitors to the city seldom see many of the courtyards. The old flagstones, fountain, statuary, shrubs, and trees all contribute to the charm of the well-concealed Old Spanish Courtyard on Madison Street.

## Bosque House Courtyard
### *619 Chartres Street*

Bartholome Bosque, a wealthy Spanish merchant, built this house in 1795. His daughter, Suzette Bosque, was Governor Claiborne's third wife.

The courtyard can be seen through the arch of the former carriageway.

*A second courtyard, in the rear of the Bosque House, has another cast-iron fountain in a round, brick base.*

*This view of the courtyard shows blooming azaleas, banana trees, and a fountain in an octagonal-shaped base.*

## Soniat House Hotel
## Entrance Courtyard
*1133 Chartres Street*

One of America's finest small hotels is hidden in a quiet residential section of the *Vieux Carré.*

In 1829 Joseph Soniat Dufossat, a prosperous plantation owner, built Soniat House Hotel as a townhouse for his large family. The hotel combines Creole style with classic Greek Revival detail. The cool, stone carriageway gives access to the picturesque entrance courtyard. The spiral staircases and galleries adorned by lace ironwork transport guests back to the New Orleans of the 1830s.

*Breakfast is served in this lovely courtyard.*

## Preservation Hall
*726 St. Peter Street*

Through the delicate wrought-iron entrance gates to Preservation Hall, one sees a tranquil patio filled with lush plants.

## Court of Two Lions
*710 Toulouse Street*

Built in 1798 by Don Juan Francisco Merieult, the Court of Two Lions gained its name from the two lions facing each other above the gateposts.

## Gallier House Courtyard
*1118-32 Royal Street*

The beautiful courtyard at Gallier House gives one a feeling of peace and serenity.

## Le Petit Theatre du Vieux Carré
## Courtyard
*616 St. Peter Street*

Le Petit Theatre du Vieux Carré was founded in 1916 by a group of theatre-loving New Orleanians. It is one of the oldest community theatres in the country and New Orleans' oldest performing arts organization.

In 1922 the present property was purchased by the theatre group, who moved here from rented space in the Pontalba Building.

The original corner building, erected in 1794 by Jean Baptiste Orso, was destroyed by fire that same year. It was rebuilt in 1797 for Don Manuel Gayoso de Limos, the last Spanish governor of Louisiana, who personally supervised the planting of flowers and shrubs in the patio to make a beautiful setting for his young wife.

After the Louisiana Purchase in 1803, the building changed ownership several times, fell into disrepair, and remained so until its acquisition by the theatre group.

## LeCarpentier-Beauregard-Keyes
## House Walled Garden
*1113 Chartres Street*

The walled garden at the side of the house was restored to its original stateliness in the 1940s by Frances Parkinson Keyes.

## Sauvinet-Lewis-Baus House
## Courtyard
### 831 Governor Nicholls Street

The charm of the courtyards at the Baus House is breathtaking. The flowering plants, including azaleas, Louisiana phlox, petunias, and geraniums, invite one to rest in these tranquil gardens.

*This view of the entrance courtyard at the Baus House was photographed from the second-floor gallery.*

### John Gauché House Courtyard
*1315 Royal Street*

Although the John Gauché House faces historic Esplanade Avenue, the entrance to the spectacular courtyard is at 1315 Royal Street and completely hidden by high walls.

The fountain in the center dominates the courtyard. Its octagonal base is surrounded by potted flowering plants. Trees and shrubs abound and delicately designed, lacy iron filigree on the railings and on the balcony guard all add to the tranquil atmosphere.

# Ironwork

Ironwork was frequently used for railings, balcony supports, fences, and gates to embellish homes built during the early days of the city of New Orleans. At that time only wrought iron was used. It was wrought or hammered by hand over a forge and anvil. Much of it was made in New Orleans; however, some better examples were shipped in from Spain. Very little carbon was used in the Spanish iron and for this reason it was more rust resistant.

Cast iron became popular in the 1830s. Molten iron was poured into molds of different designs and allowed to harden. While many New Orleans foundries could make cast iron, much of the cast iron used here was actually made in Philadelphia. The Philadelphia firm of Wood and Perot made a large quantity of iron used in the cemeteries. It is hard, brittle, and rusts more easily; therefore, to prevent rusting, it is always painted.

Both types of iron are picturesque, although wrought iron is usually more delicate and graceful. A definite lacework pattern is often made of cast iron and is stunningly beautiful. Because it was not as expensive as wrought iron, it sometimes framed the front and side of a corner building (see the LaBranche building). Wrought iron was used more sparingly.

In the cemeteries ironwork played an important part. Many tombs have cast-iron fences with gates which depict a theme or motif, such as the gate with Cupid carrying the inverted death torch. Some of the tombs have a delicately fashioned wrought iron cross above the cast-iron gate. The cross is the symbol for Christianity, the lyre for music, the weeping willow for sorrow, and the lamb for innocence. These symbols tell the stories of those within the tombs.

## Jackson Square Gate
### *Decatur Street*

Note the superb design, by Louis H. Pilié, of the massive cast-iron gate at the Decatur Street entrance to Jackson Square.

## Lower Pontalba Building Grillwork
### *Jackson Square*

Designed by Micaela Almonester, Baroness de Pontalba, the intricate cast-iron balustrades on the upper and lower Pontalba buildings incorporate the monogram *AP*, representing the names Almonester and Pontalba.

## Cabildo
### *Jackson Square*

Shown is the delicate ironwork in front of the beautifully designed Cabildo windows.

## Manheim Galleries Balcony Railing
### *409 Royal Street*

In the center of the delicate wrought-iron balcony railing are the initials *LSB,* representing the Louisiana State Bank.

## Roquette Mansion Ironwork
### *413 Royal Street*

Many times ornamental iron brackets were used to partially support balconies. The initials *DR* incorporated in the design of the railings stand for Domingue Roquette, original owner of the building.

## Royal Street Ironwork

Pictured here are two iron railings, each in a different design, with a balcony guard or *garde de frise* between them.

## Balcony Guard
### *520 Royal Street*

This is an exquisite wrought-iron balcony guard or *garde de frise* at 520 Royal Street.

## Cornstalk Hotel Gate
### *915 Royal Street*

Note the intricacy of design in the heavy cast-iron gate at the Cornstalk Hotel.

## Gallier House Ironwork
### *1118-32 Royal Street*

This delicate ironwork adorns Gallier House.

## Iron Entrance Gate
### Vieux Carré

This is the entrance to a mansion in the *Vieux Carré*. The fluted Ionic columns, carved cornice, and elegant style of this iron gate are captivating.

## Casa Correjolles Ironwork
### 715 Governor Nicholls Street

The balcony railing was made of wrought iron and the lacework shadow above the railing is from the ornamental iron grillwork edging the eaves of the balcony roof.

## Morning Glory Ironwork
### 821 Toulouse Street

This is an example of extremely delicate iron filigree in the morning glory pattern.

## Fisk-Hopkins House Gate
### *730 Esplanade Avenue*

The cast-iron gate at 730 Esplanade Avenue is quite decorative.

## John Gauché House
### *1315 Royal Street*

This is an ironwork gate at Gauché House.

*A closeup view of the iron railing pattern.*

## Nicholas M. Benachi House Gate
### *2257 Bayou Road*

Massive cast iron was used to build the delicately patterned gate at the Nicholas M. Benachi House.

## Leathers House Entrance
### *2027 Carondelet Street*

The elaborate entrance to the Leathers House is surrounded by intricate cast iron which incorporates a floral design to match the carved flowers on the door. Composite capitals, modillioned cornice, rich mouldings, and Bohemian etched glass around the door all contribute to the elegance of the mansion.

## Col. Robert H. Short Villa
## Cornstalk Fence
### 1448 Fourth Street

A cast-iron fence in cornstalk design, dating back to 1859, surrounds the Colonel Short Villa. Shown here is a fence post and part of the exquisite fence.

*The gate leading to the entrance of Colonel Short's Villa has two cornstalk gateposts made of heavy cast iron from Philadelphia.*

## Newcomb College Entrance Gate
### 1229 Broadway Street

This impressive cast-iron gate is at the Broadway Street entrance to the Newcomb College grounds. Newcomb College is affiliated with Tulane University.

## Old Spanish Custom House
*1300 Moss Street*

The cast-iron doorway gates at the Old Spanish Custom House were a later addition to the house. Gen. Andrew Jackson and Jean Lafitte met in the original part of the house, according to legend, in regard to the defense of New Orleans.

## Odd Fellows Cemetery Gate
*Canal Street at City Park Avenue*

An intricately patterned iron grillwork gate marks the entrance to Odd Fellows Cemetery.

### Dueling Oaks

The land which is now City Park was formerly part
of Allard Plantation. Louis Allard, the plantation
owner, is buried under this ancient live oak tree. It was
a favorite location for many duels fought by hot-
blooded young men in the romantic antebellum era of
the South. Here, young French and Spanish gentlemen
settled their differences with swords and pistols. This
was the field of satisfaction for wounded pride and
honor.

# Cemeteries

New Orleans is below sea level, surrounded by swampland, and subject to heavy rains. Because of these factors, in the early years the coffins were actually buried in water which was only nine to twelve inches below the surface.

Around 1800 it became compulsory to have above-ground burials in tombs which resemble small, windowless houses, close together, row-on-row, giving the effect of a miniature city. Therefore, the cemeteries are often called "Cities of the Dead." The brick tombs are plastered, whitewashed, and closed with marble tablets. The tablets list the names of the occupants and the extent of their lives. Many tombs are surrounded by ornamental iron fences with gates.

In some cases, cemetery walls are made up of burial vaults and usually stand twelve feet high and nine feet thick, which serve the double purpose of enclosing the cemetery and providing above-ground burial space at low cost.

The curiosity of visitors never fails to be aroused by the local custom of using one vault for several entombments. The vault is ready to receive another body when the remains of the present occupant are pushed to the back and the wooden casket is removed and burned.

In private, two-vault tombs, one vault above the other, the bodies are removed from the upper chamber and consigned to a receptical below the tomb when a subsequent funeral takes place.

The realization that the remains of many of the most distinguished men and women of more than a century and a half ago rest beneath the ancient tombs gives one an irrepressible feeling of melancholy brooding.

## St. Louis Cemetery #3
### *Esplanade Avenue*

The main gate at St. Louis Cemetery #3 on Esplanade Avenue is bathed in golden light at sunset.

*Sitting woefully above a tomb in St. Louis Cemetery #3 is the figure of a young mother in complete despair over the loss of her baby.*

*The Lacroix tomb in St. Louis Cemetery #3 has a unique cast-iron gate showing a weeping willow tree with doves above and lambs below reflecting sorrow and innocence.*

*Delicate-looking but durable, hand-wrought iron was used in the construction of this gate.*

*An intricate design was used in this heavy cast-iron fence.*

Another tomb which is surrounded by an iron fence.

Behind this gate of heavy cast iron sits an urn which shows an excellent example of the stonecutter's art.

This is a perfect example of seemingly fragile hand-wrought iron. The pattern is of a lyre with an exquisite cross above.

At sunset one can see what appears to be a final, glowing benediction before nightfall. Christ and the angels seem to be compassionately blessing all souls who are sleeping there.

## St. Louis Cemetery #1

On top of a cast-iron gate stands a wrought iron cross that has withstood the elements of nature throughout the years even though it is so fine in texture. It rests in front of the tomb of Paul Morphy, who was recognized at that time as the greatest chess player in the world. He was born in New Orleans in 1837 and died here in 1884.

*A praying angel-child sits on top of a decaying tomb behind an iron cross. His angelic face has been pitted by time, yet there is a quiet beauty about him.*

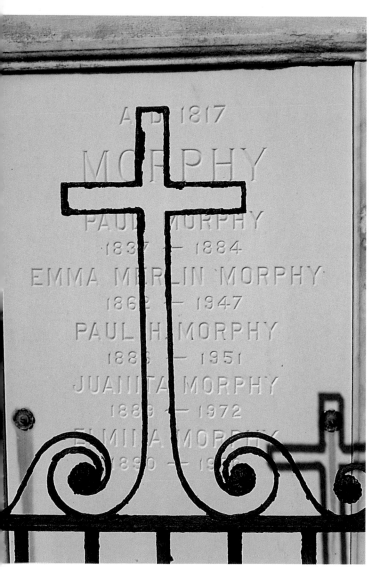

*A perfectly proportioned stone urn with interesting carvings is a tribute to the stonecutter's art.*

This shows the use of wrought iron in the lyre, which is topped with a fleur-de-lis. The fence below is of cast iron.

St. Louis Cemetery #1 is the final place of rest for many notable pioneer families. It is also the place of burial for a few notorious individuals. The Glapion family tomb is the final resting place of Voodoo Queen Marie Laveau. This tomb has been marked for good luck by the chalked X's of visitors.

Inside the rusted cast-iron fence stands this decaying, somber, old tomb, which seems to whisper of a bygone era.

The New Orleans Italian Mutual Benevolent Society, founded in 1848, built this monumental tomb in St. Louis Cemetery #1. The baroque marble circular tomb has twenty-four vaults and a receptacle in its basement closed by an iron door. It features two niches — one contains a large statue representing "Italia" and the other contains another large statue of a woman with children representing "Charity."

The well-preserved statue of a young girl in deep, sorrowful prayer sits on top of a crumbling tomb which has a beautifully executed wrought-iron cross over a cast-iron gate.

## St. Patrick Cemetery #3

The heavy cast-iron gate is fashioned in the delicate form of an angel deep in silent prayer.

*On a tomb in St. Patrick Cemetery #3 one finds a bas-relief of the anguished, mournful face of the Savior.*

## St. Patrick Cemetery #2

Cast iron was used in the construction of this gate of Gothic cathedral design.

## Greenwood Cemetery

In Greenwood Cemetery the Weeping Cupid Gate depicts the sorrow that is felt and the tears that are shed when death interrupts a love affair.

*A unique arrangement of materials is achieved by the use of both wrought iron as well as cast iron in this fence.*

*Four lyres are cut with precision on this double cast-iron gate.*

## Cypress Grove Cemetery

In Cypress Grove Cemetery an ancient live oak tree appears to be standing guard over the old graves and tombs.

*A stately tomb surrounded by an iron fence and gate is topped by an exquisitely cut urn.*

*A view of two magnificent Gothic-style tombs in Cypress Grove Cemetery.*

## Metairie Cemetery

On the door of this tomb one finds an elaborate and beautiful stone carving. Two angels seem to be ascending, one leading the other while carrying the inverted torch of death.

*Two sculptured figures guard the entrance to this impressive tomb. The stained glass at the rear is unusual.*

*In Metairie Cemetery many elaborate tombs stand. This one is in the Gothic style of architecture.*

*Pictured is a row of vaults in St. Roch Cemetery. In several cemeteries, along a border aisle, one finds a row of burial crypts which also serves as the wall of the cemetery. Constructed in the mid-nineteenth century, these vaults are historically significant for their efficient use of the land and because they foreshadowed the modern mausoleum which has become popular in the twentieth century.*

## St. Roch Cemetery

The Gothic-style St. Roch Cemetery chapel can be seen behind this crucifix. The small altar in the interior is surrounded by crutches, braces, and other medical aids left there by grateful patients who feel that they have been healed by prayer.

# Selected Bibliography

Bruns, Rev. J. Edgar, M.A., S.S.L., S.T.D. *Archbishop Antoine Blanc Memorial*. New Orleans: The Roman Catholic Church of the Archdiocese of New Orleans, 1981.

The Garden Study Club of New Orleans. *Walled Gardens of the French Quarter*. New Orleans: The Garden Study Club of New Orleans, 1974.

Guillet, John Curtis. *Louisiana's Architectural and Archaeological Legacies*. Natchitoches, La.: Northwestern State University Press, 1982.

Huber, Leonard V. *Landmarks of New Orleans*. New Orleans: Louisiana Landmarks Society and Orleans Parish Landmarks Commission, 1984.

Leavitt, Mel. *A Short History of New Orleans*. San Francisco: Lexicos, 1982.

Lynn, Stuart M. *New Orleans*. New York: Bonanza Books, 1949.

Wilson, Samuel, Jr., F.A.I.A., and Huber, Leonard V. *The St. Louis Cemeteries of New Orleans*. New Orleans: St. Louis Cathedral, 1963.